The Adventures of
KITT AND GIANNA

THIS BOOK BELONGS TO

_____

Summary: Companion coloring book to The Adventures of Kitt and Gianna: Paris, France. Join the young boy, Kitt, and his trusty Australian Labradoodle companion, Gianna, as they set out on a captivating adventure around the world. Together, they explore Paris, immersing themselves in the richness of French culture, history, and, of course, delicious food. This book is intended for children aged 3-5 years old and is designed to entertain, educate, and inspire young readers.

For permissions, inquiries, or any other requests, please contact: Kerzich Global Communications at kittandgianna@gmail.com. AMDG

ISBN: 979-8-9887369-3-6 (Paperback)
First Printing Edition 2023

KITT AND GIANNA

KITT

GIANNA

EIFFEL TOWER

NOTRE-DAME CATHEDRAL

NOTRE-DAME CATHEDRAL

EIFFEL TOWER

SEINE RIVER

LATIN QUARTER

PALACE OF VERSAILLES

MONMARTE

ARC DE TRIOMPHE

LOURVE MUSEUM

PARIS CAFE

SACRÉ COEUR

THE LATIN QUARTER

CHAMPS-ÉLYSÉES

MUSÉE D'ORSAY

SAINTE-CHAPELLE

LUXEMBOURG GARDENS

CANAL SAINT-MARTIN

LES INVALIDES

MARAIS DISTRICT

PANTHEON

PALAIS-ROYAL

LUXEMBOURG PALACE

CANAL SAINT-MARTIN

MUSÉE DE L'ARMÉE

EIFFEL TOWER

THE CITY OF LIGHT

KITT AND GIANNA